How to survive and succeed as
a SENCo in the primary school

Veronica Birkett
Marj Lautman

Acknowledgements

Veronica Birkett would like to thank:

- Marj Lautman, for her assistance with the revision of this book, and for bringing a wealth of experience and expertise to these pages;
- Cathy Griffin of LDA for her patience and quiet support;
- the many SENCos who work tirelessly on behalf of the children they support, and who make such a difference.

Marj Lautman would like to thank:

- the football teams taking part in the 2006 World Cup for keeping the men in her life, Alan, David and Daniel, entertained, giving her the opportunity to get on with the writing;
- her daughter Beth, for relinquishing the computer for a month, which to her seemed like an eternity;
- the teaching assistants at Elmore Green School in Walsall for their support and dedication and for helping her survive the role;
- Veronica Birkett for her encouragement and the LDA team for their support.

The rights of Veronica Birkett and Marj Lautman be identified as authors of this work have been asserted by them in accordance with sections 77 and 78 of the Copyright, Designs and Patents Act 1988.

How to survive and succeed as a SENCo in the primary school
MT10167
ISBN-13: 978 1 85503 421 1

Printed in the UK for LDA
Abbeygate House, East Road, Cambridge, CB1 1DB, UK

Contents

Contents

Introduction

Who will benefit from this book?

This book is written especially for special educational needs co-ordinators (SENCos) by an experienced special educational needs (SEN) consultant and a practising SENCo. It will also be useful for teachers who may be considering taking on the SENCo role. Seven years have passed since the first edition of this book, and during that time many SENCos have told us of their appreciation and enthusiasm for the practical, user-friendly approach it adopted. Since then, education in general and special needs provision in particular have been subject to many changes, so this new edition has been completely revised to reflect that.

As before, it is not the intention of the authors to portray a rosy, unrealistic picture of the position. We have aimed to present the reality – both the joys and the pitfalls – and to bring our many years of experience to the revision of this book in a way that overstretched SENCos will not find daunting. Above all, we want to show our support and respect for the many dedicated teachers who have taken on the role, and who do not always receive the acknowledgement they deserve. We hope the guidance offered in this book will help them gain greater job satisfaction and provide them with clear ideas on the management, structure and systems of the department. The ideas and suggestions here have been tried and tested in real schools, with real SENCos, and are guaranteed to enhance the efficiency of the SENCo and relieve some of the stress. This should ensure not only survival, but success and satisfaction as well.

A note about parents and carers

In some chapters we have touched on the home–school relationship for the child with SEN. We are aware that this will sometimes involve carers who are not parents. For the sake of brevity, however, we have mostly referred only to parents.

Chapter 1
Why be a SENCo?

Life's most urgent question: what are you doing for others?

Martin Luther King

Why be a SENCo? It's not a role that suits everyone, so before you read any further, consider the following list of requirements for the job of SENCo. You may be able to add some of your own. You may be able to tick off most of the points for yourself – in which case, you're probably doing a great job already. Or you may feel unable to tick off many – in which case you're probably looking for help and support. Or you may be feeling that the job isn't for you. Whatever your situation, this book will provide some ideas and strategies to help you develop in the job.

To survive and succeed in the role of SENCo, you will need to:

- be well organised;
- manage time efficiently;
- establish a team consisting of teaching assistants (TAs), the school secretary, class teachers (even though they may not be very keen to be in your team!), parents and the headteacher;
- appreciate your team;
- communicate effectively with your team and with visiting professionals;
- have a strong sense of your own worth – you are doing a very important job;
- have a sense of humour;
- make time for yourself.

The current situation

The role of the SENCo is constantly evolving and the responsibilities attached to the job are increasing. The introduction of government initiatives as part of their effort to raise standards and promote inclusion in schools has had profound implications for SENCos. The following documents are particularly significant, and you should be familiar with their contents.

- *Special Educational Needs Code of Practice* (DfES, 2002)
- *The SEN Toolkit*, additional guidance to The Code of Practice (DfES, 2001)
- *Every Child Matters: Change for children* (DfES, 2004)
- *Removing Barriers to Achievement: The government's strategy for SEN* (DfES, 2004)

The most recent of these initiatives are the SEN strategy *Removing Barriers to Achievement*, which emphasises the key role played by the SENCo, and the government's change for children programme, *Every Child Matters*, with its five important desired outcomes for nurturing and educating the whole child.

Top tip

How to remember the five outcomes

In a word: **SHEEP!**
Stay safe
Be **h**ealthy
Enjoy and achieve
Achieve **e**conomic well-being
Make a **p**ositive contribution

One of the main implications of *Every Child Matters* is the strengthening of the SENCo's relationship with other professionals involved with the child. The SENCo is now part of a multi-agency team that plans and ensures the achievement of the five outcomes for each child. In many cases, the meetings about the child will be held at school, and the SENCo works in partnership with other professionals involved with the child, sharing information. *Removing Barriers to Achievement* puts it this way:

> SENCos play a pivotal role co-ordinating provision across the school and linking class and subject teachers with SEN specialists to improve the quality of teaching and learning. We want schools to see the SENCo as a key member of the senior leadership team, able to influence the development of policies for whole school improvement
>
> (Para. 3:14)

What does the job entail?

According to the 2002 Code of Practice, a SENCo is responsible for:

- overseeing the day-to-day operation of the school's SEN policy;
- liaising with and advising fellow teachers;
- managing the TAs;
- co-ordinating provision for children with SEN;
- overseeing the records of all pupils with SEN;
- liaising with parents of children with SEN;
- contributing to the in-service training of staff;
- liaising with external agencies, including the educational psychology service and other support agencies, medical and social services and voluntary bodies.

Great opportunities to help others seldom come, but small ones surround us every day.

Anon.

What this means in reality is a lot of multi-tasking. It is rare to find a teacher in the primary sector whose sole role is being a SENCo. Most SENCos are also class teachers who somehow manage to carry out both jobs. A class-teacher SENCo has to cope not only with responsibility for a class, but also with review meetings, TA meetings, completing paperwork, monitoring the input of teachers and TAs, assessing pupils, working with individual pupils, filing and letter writing. Other tasks include persuading and helping class teachers to carry out the recommendations on Individual Education Plans (IEPs) and dealing with distressed, bewildered or even irate parents who are concerned about their child's special need – not to mention chasing up parents who have not attended review meetings. No wonder most SENCos are exhausted!

Furthermore, the job is never completed. The pile of paperwork and the number of review meetings may diminish, but they soon grow again. SENCos can never say the job is done; all they can do is find ways to manage the workload and keep on top of it. With such a responsibility, why would anyone be willing to take on the role? The answer is that the benefits of being a SENCo are plentiful.

We make a living by what we get. We make a life by what we give.

Sir Winston Churchill

The rewards of being a SENCo

Central to everything the SENCo does is the child. The personal satisfaction gained from helping a child make progress is one of the most rewarding parts of the job. Sometimes you will build up a supportive relationship that continues right through a child's time at the school.

Your role also involves finding ways to support the parents. It is rewarding to have parents who thank you and really appreciate what you do. It can be satisfying, too, when you have the opportunity to build up a relationship with parents over a number of years.

You may earn the gratitude of a class teacher who was despairing until your intervention. The SENCo should also attract the respect and support of the headteacher and governors who will be aware of how effective special needs provision affects the overall standards achieved by the school. Well-trained TAs will be an asset to the school, and their deployment in the hands of a skilled SENCo can make a considerable difference. Their involvement with the SEN arrangements may increase the reputation of the SENCo even more.

The role of SENCo provides enormous opportunities for personal and professional development. As a SENCo, you will:

- acquire, develop and share knowledge with other professionals;
- develop management skills;
- develop strategies and resources that help vulnerable groups and individuals;
- develop skills as a trainer and INSET provider.

Most of all, as a SENCo you will have the satisfaction of knowing that you are carrying out a worthwhile job which may provide long-term benefits for pupils who, without your support and guidance, could struggle throughout their school careers.

To enjoy all these benefits and not only to survive but to be effective, you have to find ways of managing the role.

Food for thought

Perhaps the biggest reward for a SENCo is knowing you can make a difference to the lives of vulnerable children. To be in a position where you have the power to have an effect on the lives of others is a privilege. In the words of Henry Brook Adams, 'A teacher affects eternity; he can never tell where his influence stops'.

Chapter 2
Evaluating your situation

I am only one. I cannot do everything but I can do something. I will not let what I cannot do interfere with what I can do.

Edward Everett Hale

Examining your performance

If you are a practising SENCo you may find it useful, before reading the rest of this book, to evaluate your current situation. If you have just taken on the role, it will, in any case, be essential for you to evaluate the arrangements you are taking over at an early stage.

The aim of the evaluation is simply to think about your role and to list the things you feel you do well, the things that you would like to do better, and the things you need to change. A possible framework for doing this is provided on page 11. You can then use this analysis to devise an action plan which will reflect your vision for the future.

Opposite is an evaluation completed by one new SENCo after working in the role for two terms. Based on this, she devised the action plan below.

SENCo Action Plan	September 10th
Action	**To be completed by:**
Train and allocate time for Mrs Smith (TA) to deal with some of the paperwork.	October 20th (half-term)
Attend two courses this term, one on hearing impairment and one on autism.	Book tomorrow for courses (December 15th and January 17th)
Ask SENCo at my neighbouring school for advice on the review meeting.	Next SENCo meeting – October 4th
Arrange meeting with head to discuss allocation of time for completing paperwork.	September 20th
Organise some in-service training for staff about special needs. Probably twilight sessions – check on dates.	(Possible dates) September 21st, September 28th, October 5th, October 19th
Make an inventory of SEN resources; Mrs Jones allocated time to help.	October 20th (half-term)
Ask the head for occasional extra time for visiting classrooms: possibly the first Tuesday of every month?	September 20th

As you work through the rest of the book, you may want to revise or add to the evaluation. We hope you will also find some ideas to add to your action plan.

OFSTED

Your action plan will also be useful if OFSTED pay you a visit. Even if you have not achieved what you were aiming for, they will see what your vision and intention are and that you have a plan for achieving them. The OFSTED inspectors will be checking on the SEN issues listed on page 10.

Evaluating your performance as a SENCo

Date:

Area	Comments
Organisation How well organised are you? Areas to consider: • Paperwork (Is it up to date and accessible?) • Record keeping • Resources • Sharing some of your workload with others e.g. TAs and school secretaries	I'm usually quite organised but am finding since I took on this role that I have paperwork everywhere and no time to do anything but the job. Need to put in additional strategies to keep on top of it. Action: Perhaps train one of my TAs to deal with some of it? Ask the head what she thinks.
Subject knowledge of SEN Do you have enough knowledge to cope with the role and with the needs of the children in your school? Are you familiar with all the areas of difficulty encountered in your school? Have all relevant adults been adequately trained in the areas they need to know about? Do you have regular meetings with other agencies who also work with the child?	I know how to complete the paperwork but need to know more about the different needs, particularly how to support children with dyslexia and autism. Also need to know how to chair an annual review meeting. Action: Look at what courses are on offer. Ask an experienced SENCo for advice on chairing.
Monitoring of planning teaching and children's progress How often do you monitor: • SEN children in their class? • teachers' SEN planning? • children's progress against their IEP targets?	I never find time to go into other classrooms. Teachers keep giving me IEPs and they are piling up in my file, but I do manage to work with children and know the progress School Action Plus children are making against their targets. Action: Ask the head for occasional extra time, maybe one day a month, when I can visit classrooms.
Use of time Do you feel you make effective use of your time? Are you allocated sufficient time out of the classroom?	This is a priority. I often feel overwhelmed by the number of tasks and often it seems I have a choice – to work with the pupils or complete the paperwork. Either I need more time, or I must give up working with the children, which will be a great shame and a loss for them as well as me. Action: Talk to the head.
Support for class teachers and TAs Do you give teachers and TAs the support they need to carry out their role?	TAs have occasional meetings to discuss how things are going, but need these more regularly. Rarely have time to talk to teachers unless I am chasing them about a missing IEP. Action: Organise some INSET on special needs for staff. A few twilight sessions?
Resources Do you know what resources you have in school? Are they adequate? Do they cater for the needs of all SEN children within school? Do other resources need to be purchased?	There are lots of resources in school and the TAs are definitely using them. Action: Make an inventory and see if there are any gaps. Don't know when I will have time!
Reviews and writing IEPs Are all children reviewed termly and are IEPs up to date?	The children's reviews always take place every term, but getting the teachers to complete the new IEPs after the review meetings is a nightmare. Action: Talk to the teachers about completing the new IEPs after the review meetings. Do they need more help or more time?

© *How to survive and succeed as a SENCo in the primary school* LDA

- Are staff aware of their responsibilities? Are they carrying them out?

- Are statutory requirements being met?

- How much money is allocated and how is it spent?

- Are the needs of all pupils with SEN being met? Do all those who require them have IEPs and are their targets being addressed?

- Have issues relating to SEN that were mentioned in the last report been implemented?

- Are resources, including the human ones, well managed?

- Is external support available and well used in the school?

- How well is the progress of pupils with SEN monitored and evaluated?

- Have TAs received training? Are they being monitored?

- Has the school taken steps to help children achieve the five outcomes of *Every Child Matters?* (Check staff know the outcomes and implications.)

- How aware is the SENCo of the strengths and weaknesses of the SEN provision?

- How are any identified weaknesses going to be addressed in the future?

- Is the SENCo familiar with the DfES document *Removing Barriers to Achievement: The government strategy for SEN?*

- How does the SENCo involve parents in the SEN process?

- How does the SENCo involve pupils in the SEN process?

And remember, the whole school is expected to share responsibility for SEN pupils; your job is to co-ordinate it.

Sources of support

You may be the only SENCo in your school, but you are not alone! There will be many other SENCos in your area, and they are an important source of help and support. In some areas, the local authority (LA) organises regular meetings where information and good practice can be shared. In other areas, groups of SENCos may organise 'cluster meetings' where they meet informally with whatever agenda is appropriate. Whatever form the meetings take, they will almost certainly help to raise your awareness of the DfES and SEN initiatives. And you'll probably be able to pick up new ideas and examples of good practice. You could even take your evaluation to an informal meeting of fellow SENCos to share ideas and help you to devise an effective action plan.

SENCo Forum:
http://lists.becta.org.uk/
mailman/listinfo/senco-forum

Another good way to communicate with other SENCos is through SENCo Forum, which is a newsgroup co-ordinated by the British Educational and Technology Communications Agency (BECTA). You can subscribe to the group through their website.

A further useful source of support is SENCO Week, a free weekly e-bulletin. To receive copies, send an email to education@electricwordpic.com with Join Senco Week as the subject line.

Evaluating your performance as a SENCo

Date:

Area	Comments
Organisation How well organised are you? Areas to consider: • Paperwork (Is it up to date and accessible?) • Record keeping • Resources • Sharing some of your workload with others e.g. TAs and school secretaries	Action:
Subject knowledge of SEN Do you have enough knowledge to cope with the role and with the needs of the children in your school? Are you familiar with all the areas of difficulty encountered in your school? Have all relevant adults been adequately trained in the areas they need to know about? Do you have regular meetings with other agencies who also work with the child?	Action:
Monitoring of planning teaching and children's progress How often do you monitor: • SEN children in their class? • teachers' SEN planning? • children's progress against their IEP targets?	Action:
Use of time Do you feel you make effective use of your time? Are you allocated sufficient time out of the classroom?	Action:
Support for class teachers and TAs Do you give teachers and TAs the support they need to carry out their role?	Action:
Resources Do you know what resources you have in school? Are they adequate? Do they cater for the needs of all SEN children within school? Do other resources need to be purchased?	Action:
Reviews and writing IEPs Are all children reviewed termly and are IEPs up to date?	Action:

Chapter 3
Identifying and addressing special needs

All children have the right to a good education and the opportunity to fulfil their potential. All teachers should expect to teach children with special educational needs and all schools should play their part in educating children from the local community, whatever their background or ability.

Removing Barriers to Achievement, DfES, 2004 (Introduction)

Every teacher has a responsibility to the children in their class who have a special need, and in part that means drawing the SENCo's attention to any pupil whom they suspect may be in that category. As the SENCo, you need to ensure that all staff are aware of exactly what is meant by 'special educational needs' and of their responsibilities to children who have them. A basic requirement of the job, therefore, is to keep the school's SEN policy up to date and to make sure it is available to all staff. If the school has a computer network linked to each classroom, then the easiest way to make sure that staff have an up-to-date copy of the policy is to put it on the network.

Initial concern

Every Child Matters highlights the importance of 'supporting closer working between universal services like schools and specialist services so that children with additional needs can be identified earlier and supported effectively'. The Code of Practice, too, emphasises the need to identify pupils at the earliest possible time (Para. 5:11). There can be no doubt of the wisdom of this guidance. However, the Code also emphasises the need for teachers to support less able pupils effectively within the classroom, so that most of them will not need to be identified as having a special educational need requiring anything additional to or different from the differentiated curriculum. So, before deciding whether a child might need to be identified as having special needs, it is worth considering whether any aspect of what is provided could be creating difficulties. As the Code says:

> Schools should not assume that children's learning difficulties always result solely, or even mainly, from problems within the child. A school's own practices make a difference – for good or ill.
>
> (Para. 5:18)

This message has been reinforced by *Removing Barriers to Achievement*:

> Difficulties in learning often arise from an unsuitable environment – inappropriate grouping of pupils, inflexible teaching styles or inaccessible curriculum materials – as much from individual children's physical, sensory or cognitive impairments. Children's emotional and mental health needs may also have a significant impact on their ability to make the most of the opportunities in school, as may family circumstances.
>
> (Para. 2:1)

Teachers concerned about a pupil or pupils in their class should therefore, as a first step in response to concern, consider the following questions:

- Is differentiation adequate for all pupils in all subjects?
- Are learning support assistants skilfully deployed in the support of low-achieving pupils?
- Are suitable resources available to meet the needs of all pupils within the classroom environment?
- Are issues regarding low self-esteem, often experienced by low achievers, taken into account?
- Do I know what kind of learners the pupils are?
- Do lessons take account of children's different learning styles?
- Am I able to identify the particular area of special need experienced by individual pupils?
- Am I using accelerated learning approaches?
- Is the classroom environment inclusive for all pupils?
- Are parents sufficiently involved and informed of their children's progress?
- Does planning, particularly in literacy and numeracy, take sufficient account of the individual learning targets of individual pupils?
- Are questions being differentiated and is the 'no hands up' strategy used sometimes?
- What support is available to help me decide if a pupil has an SEN?

As SENCo, you might suggest these questions when a teacher first reports their concerns about a child. Or, better still perhaps, you could make the list part of the school's SEN policy.

If the class teacher feels that, having taken account of all that may be impinging on a struggling pupil's ability to learn, there is still cause for concern, then – in consultation with the SENCo – they have to decide whether to take some initial action. This clearly involves professional judgement and knowledge of the child.

Before any child is officially identified as having SEN and thus placed at School Action, they will need to be recorded as causing concern.

Before any child is officially identified as having SEN and thus placed at School Action, they will need to be recorded as causing concern. It is useful to have a system to record and keep track of such children. Again, some LAs have paperwork in place for this – sometimes called a Notification of Concern or a Record of Concern. If not, then it is a good idea for the school to have its own system of documentation, which could be along the lines of the one on page 17. We shall refer to this documentation as the Record of Concern.

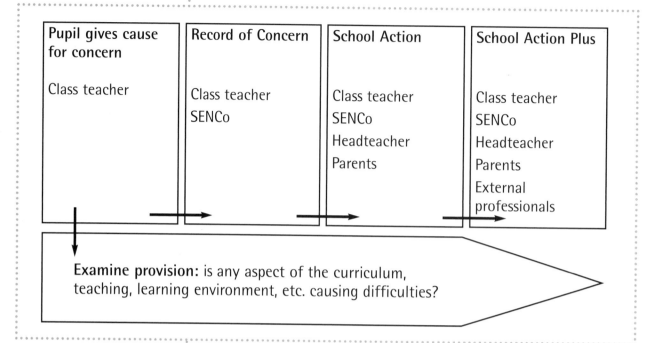

Pupil gives cause for concern	Record of Concern	School Action	School Action Plus
Class teacher	Class teacher SENCo	Class teacher SENCo Headteacher Parents	Class teacher SENCo Headteacher Parents External professionals

Examine provision: is any aspect of the curriculum, teaching, learning environment, etc. causing difficulties?

Putting concern on record

The preliminary stage in the process of identifying a child with SEN – which could be called the 'period of concern' – is a very important one. When the Record of Concern has been created, the child is observed, targeted and monitored. The class teacher gathers evidence so that if the decision is made later to move the pupil to School Action, the information is available to help the SENCo and class teacher devise the first individual education plan (IEP). The teacher will also inform the parents of their concern. The child may need to be on the Record of Concern for up to two terms before a decision can be made.

The Record of Concern is very useful in helping to focus on a child's particular needs. Targets put into place at this time may mean that some pupils will never need to move to School Action; early intervention will help them to catch up. Listed below are some particular situations where it is more likely that some pupils will become a cause for concern. Early intervention in these situations may mean that many of these pupils will never need to be identified as having a special educational need or be moved to School Action.

Foundation Stage

In the Foundation Stage, pupils may display immaturity that affects their learning or behaviour. After a few months of being in school, and possibly on a Record of Concern, these problems may well have disappeared. It would not be appropriate to record such pupils as having a special educational need.

Pupils new to the school

It would not be appropriate to intervene on behalf of a new pupil who enters the school with apparent difficulties; they may, after a period of settling down, begin to cope well.

"Pupils may display immaturity that affects their learning or behaviour."

Every Child Matters recognises that 'pupil performance and well being go hand in hand'.

Traumas and health problems

Every Child Matters recognises that 'pupil performance and well being go hand in hand. Pupils can't learn if they don't feel safe or if health problems are allowed to create barriers'. Health problems or trauma at home – such as parental break-up – may be the cause of a child's problems at school. Again, the effect may be temporary; awareness and understanding of the situation will help the child, and may be the only intervention needed.

The beginning of the school year

A teacher taking over a new class at the beginning of the year may be tempted to identify pupils as having special educational needs because of their low levels of attainment in literacy, numeracy or both. In this case, the history of the class must be borne in mind; some classes have suffered under unfortunate circumstances. If, for example, their teacher has been absent on long-term sick leave, they may have had a series of supply teachers. Or they may be struggling as a result of poor or inadequate teaching. It is amazing how some pupils, once in the hands of a competent and reliable teacher, may suddenly take off and lose their potential to be considered as children with special educational needs. Furthermore, children do not learn at an even rate; they sometimes reach a plateau before taking off again. Teachers need to consider all these factors when looking at the progress of children in their class; they may then decide to place some children on a Record of Concern. They also need to ensure that they are helping pupils achieve the five outcomes.

Top tip

Helping teachers to understand the process
The Record of Concern process may be used as the focus of an INSET session (see page 49) to help teachers understand the process involved and avoid premature or delayed identification.

Moving to a decision

The evidence gathered on the Record of Concern helps to answer the question: Does the child need to be moved to School Action? It supports the teacher in helping to identify exactly what constitutes SEN. It should help to avoid identifying pupils too early or, sadly, too late through confusion rather than neglect. Teachers will be aware of pupils who are not making the progress expected, despite the additional differentiation and monitoring offered by the Record of Concern. At this stage, more formal action will need to be taken. For example, a Reception child who should be familiar with a certain number of words by the end of the summer term, and knows less than half of them, needs some early intervention. The child must be identified officially as having a special need, and additional targets and support must be offered by placing the pupil at School Action.

There are, of course, no exact criteria for placing children at School Action, but the Code suggests making use of the following information:

- their performance monitored by the teacher as part of ongoing observation and assessment;
- the outcomes from baseline assessments;
- their progress against the objectives specified in the National Literacy and Numeracy Frameworks;
- their performance against the level descriptions within the National Curriculum at the end of a key stage;
- standardised screening or assessment tools.

(Para. 5:13)

Checking on the child's attendance should be added to this list. A child with poor attendance may have gaps in their learning, but this does not necessarily constitute a special educational need. Extra tuition, not identification, would be needed in this case. The critical indicator must be whether the gap between the achievement, progress and behaviour of the pupil and their peers is widening. The Code indicates the following possible triggers for School Action:

- makes little or no progress even when teaching approaches are targeted, particularly in a child's identified areas of weakness;
- shows signs of difficulty in developing literacy or numeracy skills which result in poor attainment in some curriculum areas;
- presents persistent emotional or behavioural difficulties which are not ameliorated by the behaviour management techniques usually employed by the school;
- has sensory or physical problems and continues to make little or no progress despite the provision of specialist equipment;
- has communication and/or interaction difficulties and continues to make little or no progress despite the provision of a differentiated curriculum.

(Para. 5:44)

Once the decision has been made to offer the child the support of School Action, parents should be informed and invited into school to discuss the next steps. It is at this stage that the SENCo becomes much more involved, and the name of the identified child will be added to the school SEN profile, which lists those pupils with special educational needs. If the Record of Concern has been completed, the SENCo will have the assessments to help plan, with the class teacher, the support and the next steps for the pupil. If not, further assessments may need to be carried out by the SENCo. The pupil has now been identified as having a special or additional need and has become involved in what is referred to as the 'graduated process'.

Record of Concern

To be completed by the class teacher

Date   _____

Pupil   _____

Class   _____   Age _____   Date of birth _____

Teacher   _____

Concerns (please give brief details of main areas of concern)

Learning targets	Strategies and support	Progress	Time (period the targets are in place)

Record of Concern

Parents' or carers' views (to be collected during the period of concern)	
Child's views	
Strengths	

Tick evidence supplied to support the proposed move to School Action or removal from the Record of Concern.

Evidence	
Reading age	
National Curriculum tests	
Assessments	
Medical notes	
Attendance	
Behaviour	

Action needed	
School Action	
Removal from Record of Concern	
Advice from Literacy or Numeracy Co-ordinator	

Chapter 4
The graduated approach

The graduated approach recognises that children learn in different ways and can have different kinds or levels of SEN. So increasingly, step by step, specialist expertise can be bought in to help the school with the difficulties that a child may have.

Special Educational Needs: A guide for parents and carers, DfES (2001)

The partnership between school and home is important for all pupils, but even more so when the child has been identified as having SEN. School and home have to work together on the identified learning targets if the child is going to make progress. In this chapter, we will look at how this works at each stage of the 'graduated process', beginning with the child at School Action.

School Action

When a child on a Record of Concern has been closely monitored and has followed a differentiated programme but has failed to make the progress expected, the school must take additional action. The child's name should be added to the list of pupils in the school who have SEN (some schools call this list a profile) and the child should be placed at School Action. At this point, the SENCo, with the help of the class teacher, has to gather all the information available about the child. This will include:

- ● medical information;
- ● assessment information;
- ● school reports;
- ● SATs results;
- ● records of attendance;
- ● any other relevant information.

With this information, the school is in a position to devise an appropriate IEP with specific learning and behaviour targets to suit the needs of the child.

If there has been contact between school and home during the 'concern period', the invitation to come in to school to discuss the decision to place the child at School Action and the child's first IEP should not come as a surprise to the parents. Even so, it needs to be handled with sensitivity. A written invitation is required, but this can be accompanied by a phone call from the SENCo or class teacher, or a brief word with the parent when they come to school at the end of the day. Of course, if you are speaking to a parent at school to invite them to an SEN meeting, do respect confidentiality. Try not to speak in earshot of other parents.

A template letter to parents can be kept on the computer, to be personalised and printed off as needed. It is always helpful to add a reply slip to the bottom.

"Oh, Mrs Johnson, may I have a word in the classroom?"

Dear [parent/carer's name(s)]

A meeting to review the progress of [child's name] will take place on:

[Date]
[Time]
[Place]

Please fill in the reply slip, and return it to the school as soon as possible. If the date is not convenient, please also phone the school on [school number] to arrange another appointment.
Many thanks.

Yours sincerely,

Class teacher

The IEP

Before the first meeting, the IEP must be drawn up, in consultation with the child. The Code of Practice says that the IEP should contain:

- the short-term targets set for the child;
- the teaching strategies to be used;
- the provision to be put in place;
- when the plan is to be reviewed;
- success and/or exit criteria;
- outcomes (to be recorded when IEP is reviewed).

(Para. 5:50)

IEP Writer:
www.learnhow
publications.co.uk

The IEP should state the child's main areas of need, for example speech and language, behaviour or literacy. ICT can help you save a lot of time when writing IEPs. You may be able to use a program specifically for creating IEPs, for example *IEP Writer*, or you may be able to put a version of your local authority's paperwork on the computer.

The IEP should record only targets that are additional to or different from the differentiated curriculum which is already in place for all children. The targets should be:

- ◗ SMART: Specific, Measurable, Achievable, Realistic and Time-related;
- ◗ only three or four in number;
- ◗ related to the areas of need for the child: communication, literacy, numeracy, behaviour and social skills;
- ◗ monitored regularly;
- ◗ reviewed termly.

Having said all that, it may be that not every pupil at School Action requires an IEP. As part of the drive to cut down on paperwork, the government has removed the requirement for IEPs at School Action, stating that: 'Many schools feel they must keep elaborate IEPs, sometimes as a result of the policy of the local authority. There is no statutory requirement for schools to prepare separate IEPs for all pupils with SEN as long as they have sound arrangements for monitoring their progress in conjunction with the child and their parents.' Nevertheless, schools must be certain that the needs of such pupils are met and provide evidence that this is so. SEN pupils without IEPs will need very clear, timed, specific targets, and you must be certain that the school targets reflect their needs. In the case of pupils without IEPs, there would still be a termly meeting to discuss progress and set new targets, and both parents and pupils must be very clear about these. There would also need to be records of what School Action took place that was in addition to that provided for the rest of the class.

The Code suggests that IEPs should be reviewed termly and that one of the reviews each year could coincide with a routine parents' evening. This, of course, would depend on the wishes of the parent and the anticipated complexity of the review. Review meetings should be informal, and the views of the parent and child should be considered.

Involving the child with target setting

Whenever possible, the child should be involved in setting their own targets. After the IEP has been devised, the teacher should help the pupil compile their own list of targets by translating the language of the targets into words the pupil can understand. For example, 'to learn the first 10 high-frequency words from the National Literacy Strategy' could be written down by the pupil as 'to learn 10 new words'. It may also be necessary to make the targets more specific. So in this example, it would be helpful for the child to know, specifically, which ten words they need to learn.

A pupil record sheet is a useful way of doing this. It ensures the pupil knows exactly what the targets are and when they need to have achieved them. It also helps to give them ownership of the targets and a greater incentive to achieve. The targets sheet can be examined regularly, with the pupil ticking the targets off as they are achieved. This keeps the targets clearly in view and helps to keep the pupil on task.

Involving the child in setting their own targets can be very beneficial. But don't promise anything until you know their requests. Targets actually requested by children include: 'to read without wearing glasses', 'to run faster than my friends in the playground' and 'not to have to have any targets or support'!

My Targets

My name is   _____

I am in class   _____

Today's date is   _____

These are my targets:

1
_____
_____

2
_____
_____

3
_____
_____

4
_____
_____

I think I will be able to reach these targets and I hope to achieve them by

_____

Signed   _____

Shared with   _____

Top tip

Survival tip: keep copies

When the IEP has been devised, it's a good idea to make at least four photocopies:
- one for your records;
- one for the class teacher;
- one for the parents to keep;
- one for the TA, if one is involved.

The target sheet should be kept by the class teacher in their SEN ring binder (see page 40). The pupil and TA should also have copies. The sheet can be used as a kind of contract between the pupil and class teacher or TA, and can be examined at regular intervals to monitor progress. If the pupil seems a long way from achieving the targets, it can be a useful means of drawing their attention to the lack of progress and discussing possible reasons.

Review meetings

Review meetings should be held once a term to evaluate the child's progress, as defined by whether or not the targets have been achieved. Again, the child should be involved. Using a review sheet like the one below can be a good way to gather their views and to help them reflect on their achievements. This process can help a child develop greater self-awareness and recognise what they are good at as well as the things they find more difficult. They may realise that they need to change some aspect of their approach or attitude to work or relationships to gain more success in school. The process can also help all who work with the child to recognise that there are things they may need to change in the future.

My Review

Name   _____

Date   _____

The best thing about school is

What I don't like about school is

The work I like doing best is

I would like help next term with

Signed   _____

Shared with   _____

Once a pupil has been identified as requiring School Action, it is very important for all those involved with the provision for special needs to be aware of the implications and responsibilities of their role.

Roles and responsibilities at School Action

As SENCo, your first task may be to ensure that all members of staff are fully aware of the SEN policy, of the graduated response the school has in place and of what is expected of the staff. So the key question is: Who does what, why and when? Here is a summary of the roles at School Action.

The class teacher:

- ❍ is responsible for the initial identification of a pupil's special needs through ongoing assessment and observation of classroom practice;

- ❍ must inform the SENCo of their concern and provide them with the relevant information to help establish whether the pupil's needs are in fact different from or additional to the those met by the differentiated class curriculum and whether the needs are best met through the introduction of School Action;

Information for a SENCo devising an IEP

Thomas Scott   Year 6
- Can read six words
- Unable to write his name
- Is late for school every day
- Fights in playground daily
- Will not stay in seat
- Keeps trying to leave the classroom
- Seems unable to understand simple instructions

- ❍ should supply the SENCo with all the information necessary to assist them in devising an effective IEP for the pupil, which will be in addition to an already differentiated curriculum;

- ❍ should write the child's IEP in consultation with the SENCo and in discussion with the child and parents;

- ❍ discusses with the parents ways they can contribute to the child's achieving the targets on the IEP;

- ❍ arranges and attends subsequent review meetings with the SENCo, parents and, if appropriate, the child, until such time as the school decides that the pupil no longer requires School Action or that the pupil needs to move on to gain support from School Action Plus;

- ❍ informs the SENCo of any problems that arise between reviews;

- ❍ organises the timetable, class grouping and available resources so that the pupil receives all possible support to reach the targets;

- ❍ reads through the agreed targets on the IEP and asks the pupil to fill in a targets sheet which will act as an informal contract between teacher and pupil;

- ❍ maintains ongoing liaison with the pupil on progress;

- ❍ plans and differentiates for the pupil's needs.

The SENCo:

- ❍ must advise the class teacher about the decision to intervene on the pupil's behalf through School Action;

- ❍ if possible, makes an informal assessment of the pupil's needs as well as collecting all available assessments and other information about them already held by the school;

○ provides the class teacher with an SEN file for the purpose of keeping together all information on the SEN pupils in that class along with other essential SEN information;

○ completes official SEN paperwork and distributes to the class teacher any paperwork which it may be more appropriate for them to complete;

○ must inform the parents of the school's concerns and invite them by letter to a meeting with the SENCo and the teacher, to discuss those concerns and to be informed of the decision to introduce School Action;

○ devises the IEP in close co-operation with the class teacher, using the results of the informal assessment or other test results, along with information provided by the class teacher;

○ sends a copy of the IEP to parents should they fail to respond to the initial invitation and follow-up phone call to meet the teacher and SENCo;

○ organises a file in which to keep all the information regarding the pupil;

○ informs the parents of the LA Parent Partnership services, which should ensure that the parent has access to information, advice and guidance relating to the educational needs of their child;

○ sends a copy of the IEP to the parents after the review meetings;

○ ensures that there are adequate resources within the school to meet the needs of all pupils who are experiencing difficulties;

○ attends the review meetings and advises the parents how they may help at home;

○ suggests possible resources or strategies that could be used in support of the child, both in class and at home;

○ provides the parents with a copy of the school's inclusion and special needs policy or shows them the relevant part of the school prospectus, which should include a summary of the SEN policy;

○ where appropriate, arranges for the child to receive support from a TA;

○ contacts outside agencies for informal advice and further information if needed;

○ makes occasional class visits and examines records kept by the class teacher to monitor the pupil's progress;

○ makes the decision, after a reasonable period of time and in agreement with the class teacher and parents, that the pupil no longer requires School Action or that the pupil needs to proceed to School Action Plus.

There are only two lasting bequests we can give our children... one is roots, the other, wings.

Stephen Covey

Once the parent has been told of the school's concern, they will be aware that the school is closely monitoring the progress of their child. Once the school has decided that the child would benefit from the extra support provided by School Action, parents must be informed and the school must handle the matter with sensitivity. Some parents are distressed when they hear of the school's decision because they do not want their child to be identified as 'different'. Most parents, however, welcome the help and will often admit that they too have been worried about their child's progress.

In some cases, parents themselves initiate the process. They may feel upset if the school fails to accept that their child has a special need and is not willing to make the extra provision that identification implies.

To identify a child as having SEN is a significant step, and the impact of the decision for the parents may be far greater than the school realises. For example, it has been known for some parents to lose interest in their child: this is no longer the bright and accomplished child they had dreamed of having. Conversely, some parents apply too much pressure in order to 'bring them up to scratch'.

The full co-operation of parents is important for the smooth running of the process.

The full co-operation of parents is important for the smooth running of the process. If this isn't forthcoming, it may result in the whole SEN process being delayed. And if a child does not feel supported by their parents, their motivation to achieve their targets may be affected. In such cases, the support of the teacher becomes even more important; it may not wholly compensate for lack of interest and support from home, but it helps.

The parents:
- provide the class teacher and the SENCo with any relevant information, including details about the child's health, early development and behaviour at home;
- give consent for the school to make a request to put the child onto the next phase of support, should this be needed;
- sign and return copies of any home–school liaison arrangements;
- co-operate with any arrangements made with out-of-school professionals;
- offer support and encouragement to the child;
- supervise the child at home when doing any work which will help the child achieve the set targets, as agreed at the review meetings;
- inform the class teacher or SENCo about any problems that occur between meetings;
- attend all the review meetings;
- ensure their child is adequately nourished and clothed, has adequate sleep and rest and is fully equipped for school;
- provide the school with their views on the child's progress and the support given.

The Code says that from the start all children should be involved in the decision-making process, in the development of the IEP and in setting targets. The child's personal targets sheet will help with this. It also helps if we view the child's special needs as a challenge rather than a problem. They are then more likely to feel encouraged and supported. We know for ourselves that our most effective advisers and helpers don't take over, but simply show us the way. It is the same with pupils with special needs. The school, class teacher, SENCo, TA, and hopefully the parents, will all do their bit, but they need to know the child's answer to the question: What are you going to do?

The pupil:

- ❍ is asked to contribute to the targets on the IEP;
- ❍ is invited to attend the review meeting — or part of it, if this is advisable;
- ❍ completes a targets sheet to act as a contract between them and the teacher;
- ❍ is told the outcome of review meetings, even if the parents do not attend.

It is all part of the subtle process of getting the pupil to take responsibility for their own future. This shift of responsibility needs to be reflected in the language we use. As we talk to the pupil about their progress, it is good to use questions and comments such as:

How do you feel you have got on this term with your targets?

We are so pleased with you. You have worked really well, James, and you have achieved all the targets!

How do you feel you got on this term with your targets? You did not achieve all of them. Did you find them difficult? What do you think we can do to help you achieve them?

How do you think you could help yourself? Could it be that you have had too much time away from school?

Let's look at ways of helping you achieve your targets. We can work together to make sure you reach them.

Be prepared for some weird and wonderful excuses when targets are not achieved! For example:

The dog has been sick so I was too worried to do my work.

My mum won't let me do it.

I have been on holiday.

Fayed won't let me get on with the work.

I keep losing my homework on the way home.

My baby sister ripped it up.

The pupil should also:

- ❍ reflect on the work over the term by completing a review sheet (this could also be done half-termly so that progress and problems can be sorted more quickly);
- ❍ be aware, through regular informal contact with the teacher and SENCo, that there is ongoing interest in their progress towards the achievement of the targets.

"Well, the dog ate my work... and then a robber came to the house and stole all the pencils... and now I've hurt my knee so I can't write."

Survival tip: talk to the pupil

Try to make time to talk to all SEN pupils and look at their work in class before a review. It is useful to compare it with the peer group.

Top tip

School Action Plus

Of the pupils who are placed at School Action, most will overcome their difficulties without any further measures being taken. If after a period of time (normally after at least two IEPs and reviews) the pupil is not making the progress expected, the school may need to consider moving them on to the next phase, School Action Plus.

The Code identifies triggers for School Action Plus as follows:

> The child:
> • continues to make little or no progress in specific areas over a long period;
> • continues to work at National Curriculum levels substantially below that expected of children of a similar age;
> • continues to have difficulty developing literacy and mathematics skills;
> • has emotional or behavioural difficulties which substantially and regularly interfere with the child's own learning or that of the class group, despite having an individualised behaviour management programme;
> • has sensory or physical needs, and requires additional specialist equipment or regular advice or visits by a specialist service;
> • has ongoing communication or interaction difficulties that impede the development of social relationships and cause substantial barriers to learning.
>
> (Para. 5:56)

School Action Plus is the time when the school calls in the aid of external agencies. The external services should advise teachers about IEPs, strategies and resources that are available for the child. They may act in an advisory capacity or provide an assessment. Or it may be that teaching support will be available from outside professionals. In this case the permission of the parents must be sought. It is mandatory for all LAs to employ educational psychologists and education welfare officers, and there should also be a range of other outside agencies that may be called upon to support the school with further advice or assessments. These include:

- behaviour support service;
- learning support service (for pupils with mild to moderate learning difficulties);
- hearing impaired service;
- visual impaired service;
- pre-school service;
- hospital teaching service;
- speech and language therapists;
- clinical psychologists;
- child psychiatrists;
- paediatric occupational therapists;
- paediatricians;
- physiotherapists.

The list is not exhaustive, and there may be other personnel from the health authority and the social services department who could be called upon to provide advice and support. As the SENCo, you should also be aware of and have information about voluntary organisations such as bereavement counselling or single-parent support groups. Before any outside advice can be sought, parental permission is required. This needs to be given in writing, perhaps using a form such as the following.

Permission from parents to seek advice from outside agencies

I have been informed by [name of SENCo]
that the school wishes to seek involvement from [name of outside agency]
for advice and support with regard to my child [name of child]

I give my full permission for this consultation.

Signed　　　　_____

Name　　　　_____

Date　　　　_____

Roles and responsibilities at School Action Plus

When a pupil is moved to School Action Plus, the roles and responsibilities of the parent and pupil are the same as for School Action, but there are additional responsibilities for the class teacher and SENCo.

The class teacher:

○ continues to support the pupil in the same way as for School Action, incorporating any extra help and resources as specified by the IEP on behalf of the pupil, attending reviews and taking account of the advice of the outside agency involved.

The SENCo:

○ informs the school and parents of the decision to initiate School Action Plus on behalf of the pupil and seeks the parents' permission for the involvement of outside agencies;

○ fills in the relevant paperwork for the LA, who will decide if School Action Plus is appropriate;

- works in close co-operation with the outside agency selected to provide advice and support for the pupil, class teacher and parent;
- devises the IEP in co-operation with the outside agency, class teacher and parent;
- seeks advice from the literacy and numeracy co-ordinators as necessary;
- completes all the relevant paperwork.

Statutory assessment

For a very small minority of pupils, progress through School Action Plus may not provide adequate or appropriate support. In this case, the school – after consultation with the parents, class teacher and outside agency – has to make a request for a statutory assessment (as described in the Code of Practice, paragraph 5:62). Parents also have the right to request an assessment at this stage. Alternatively, the request may come from social services or other agencies who have had close contact with the child. In the period when the LA is considering the request, the pupil should continue to be supported through School Action Plus.

Roles and responsibilities at statutory assessment

The time from the request for a statutory assessment to the issue of the statement should be no more than 26 weeks.

The local authority considers the evidence and must decide, within six weeks, if they are willing to carry out a statutory assessment. The time from the request for a statutory assessment to the issue of the statement should be no more than 26 weeks.

Should the request for assessment be refused, the parents will be contacted and the reasons given for the decision. Parents have the right to take the matter to an SEN tribunal, provided the school made the request or it was requested under section 328 or 329 (see Code Para. 7:71).

The headteacher, before referring the pupil for statutory assessment, is responsible for ensuring the school can provide written evidence for the following, as laid down by the Code of Practice:

- the school's action through School Action and School Action Plus;
- the pupil's IEPs;
- records of regular reviews and their outcomes;
- the pupil's health, including medical history where relevant;
- National Curriculum levels;
- attainment in literacy and numeracy;
- educational and other assessments, for example from an advisory specialist or an educational psychologist;
- views of the parent and the pupil;
- involvement of other professionals;
- any involvement by the social services or education welfare service.

(Para. 5:64)

The class teacher will proceed as for School Action Plus while the LA is in the process of making the decision.

The SENCo:

● collates all previous information on the progress of the child;

● sends this information to the LA with the appropriate paperwork, requesting a statutory assessment;

● continues to monitor and review the pupil's progress with the class teacher and outside agency.

Pupils with statements

Once the decision has been made to issue a pupil with a statement, there are further responsibilities for the class teacher and SENCo – and for the TAs.

Roles and responsibilities at statement
The class teacher:

● follows the procedure for the school-based provision, supervising the pupil's timetable to accommodate the hours allocated to the pupil from a TA.

The SENCo:

● follows the same procedures as identified for the school-based stages, ensuring regular IEPs are prepared and review meetings take place, and in addition must submit written reports on the pupil's progress for the annual review meetings specified by the LA;

● ensures that review meetings are held within the time specified by the LA;

● requests before the review, on behalf of the headteacher, written advice from the child's parents and any other person who has involvement with the child;

● circulates, two weeks before the meeting, copies of all the written advice received, to all parties invited to the annual review;

● chairs the review meeting following the agenda;

● monitors the progress of the pupil (making use of the SEN file) and supports class teachers and TAs with advice and resource suggestions;

● asks TAs to fill in monitoring sheets to record the progress of the pupil towards their IEP targets (see page 33 for a form that may be used);

● ensures that the TA is provided with adequate training and information to carry out their role effectively.

Teaching assistants have become a very important part of the SEN graduated process. Their presence in the classroom and all the extra help and support they give to both teachers and children mean that pupils are less likely to struggle with their work and develop learning difficulties in the first place. For pupils with a statement, the role of the TA can be crucial in helping them achieve their IEP targets. Indeed, the terms of the statement usually determine that a TA be allocated to a pupil for a number of hours each week. It is important that the TA keeps records of the work carried out with the child, particularly if that child has a statement. The completed record sheets may be used as a focus by the TA when required to write a report on the pupil's progress for review meetings. The record sheet on page 33 may be useful not only for recording the pupil's progress, but also for the SENCo and teacher to monitor the work of the TA.

... inspections show that the quality of teaching in lessons with teaching assistants is better than in lessons without them.

Teaching Assistants in Primary Schools, Ofsted (2002)

Annual reviews

One of the keys to successful annual review meetings is organisation. Below is a checklist for annual reviews and a model agenda for a review meeting. If you keep an electronic copy of the agenda, it can be easily updated and changed for individual pupils.

Checklist for annual review

- Have invitations been written and sent to all who need to attend?
- Have replies been received?
- Is an interpreter needed?
- Has the IEP been reviewed?
- Have the child's views been sought?
- Have the parents' views been sought?
- Has the class teacher written a report?
- Have the outside agencies' reports been received?
- Have the reports been photocopied?

Model of an agenda for a review meeting

Annual review meeting for [pupil's name]   Date

- Welcome and introductions
- Apologies
- Explanation of the purpose of the meeting: to review [pupil's] progress, over the past [period of time] towards meeting the overall objectives of their statement. To make decisions for the future by considering the following questions:

  - Are the terms of the statement still appropriate?
  - Does the child still need the protection of a statement?
  - Is this school the most appropriate educational setting?
  - Does the child need more or less allocated TA time?
  - Does the child require additional resources not currently available in the school?

- School reports
- Report from class teacher
- Discussion of IEP targets
- Reports from other agencies (e.g. educational psychologists)
- Support services reports (e.g. health)
- Parents' views delivered by [name of person]
- Pupil's views delivered by [name of person]
- Consideration of the appropriateness of the statement
- Does the statement remain appropriate? Does anything need changing?
- Consideration of further action required and by whom
- New targets for the coming year
- Recommendations of the meeting
- Next review date

Making reviews manageable

It is helpful to choose one week in the term when all the reviews are held, and to do this with the class teachers at a staff meeting. If your SENCo time can be organised, choose one day for all School Action Plus and termly statement reviews (although the annual review, clearly, will take place a year from the previous one). The benefits of this system for you are as follows:

○ All review paperwork is completed at the same time.

○ It is easy to see if a review has not been completed.

○ It means that all the review paperwork and new reviews are being handed to the SENCo during a set period, so it can then all be filed at once in the SEN filing cabinet.

If you don't have a single review week, you can end up having paperwork handed in continuously by teachers over a term and it becomes much harder to keep track of which reviews have been completed. You can then end up chasing round after paperwork rather than getting on with more important things like getting home at a reasonable time. Choosing a week for all reviews means you are extremely busy for one week, but you can organise your other commitments in school around this so that your workload is manageable. For example, if you are SENCo and a Year 2 teacher, don't choose the weeks you are testing and tasking for SATs as your review week.

Pupil record sheet

Pupil's name _____ Class _____

Date	Activity	Observations	Staff

Chapter 5
Managing special needs provision

No man is an island, entire of itself

John Donne

As the SENCo, you do not stand alone; every teacher is involved with special needs and you need the support of every member of staff. Your success will depend on the delegation of responsibility for special needs provision to all those involved, but it will also depend on how well you have organised the provision and how accessible and comprehensible this is to the rest of the staff. So what is the best way to organise the vast amount of paperwork and resources that accompany the SENCo role? In this chapter, we will look at some tried-and-tested ways of efficiently managing, monitoring and co-ordinating the special needs provision within the school. The ideas – which are really just common sense – have come from years of experimenting with different processes. And this is what we have found works best.

The equipment you will need includes:
- ❍ a four-drawer filing cabinet;
- ❍ a computer;
- ❍ some shelves or other storage space for SEN resources;
- ❍ an SEN ring binder for every teacher in the school;
- ❍ a 'kit' of essential materials and equipment for working with pupils;
- ❍ a large diary.

The filing cabinet

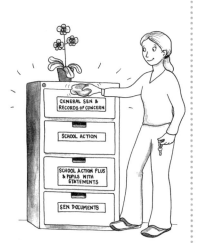

To keep all the essential documents together, you will need a filing cabinet with four drawers. It will contain, amongst other things, confidential pupil records and paperwork – so it must be lockable. It should be sited in a place where you can get to it easily at any time (not in the headteacher's office, for example). The contents should be filed using a clear, easy-to-manage system, such as the one suggested here.

Top tip

Survival tip
Make sure you have two keys for the filing cabinet, and keep them in a safe place. Access to the cabinet should be restricted to the SENCo, the headteacher and the school secretary. Teachers and TAs must be provided with copies of all relevant information.

First drawer: General SEN and Records of Concern
Records of Concern

At the front of the top drawer (so easily accessible) is a good place to keep the file for pupils who have been identified as a cause for concern. This will contain Records of Concern for pupils who are under scrutiny by the class teacher, but whose needs do not yet warrant being moved to School Action. Class teachers should keep the Record of Concern and evidence collected for each pupil in their class in their SEN ring binder; you should also keep copies in the Records of Concern file in the filing cabinet.

The SEN profile

The SEN profile should list the names of all pupils who have been placed at School Action and at School Action Plus and who have statements.

The SEN profile should list the names of all pupils who have been placed at School Action and at School Action Plus and who have statements. The information for each pupil should include their name, class and date of birth. This record should also be kept on the computer, with both the electronic and the hard copies being updated regularly.

There should also be a file with records of pupils who no longer need the support of School Action, whom you will be monitoring.

Paperwork blanks

Official paperwork varies from authority to authority, but it is very important that you are familiar with the paperwork required by yours, and have an understanding of their policies, procedures and expectations for the SEN process. Failure to get to grips with this could result in a delay in getting the needs of pupils addressed. This section of the drawer would also include the school's own SEN paperwork.

Second drawer: School Action

For each pupil at School Action you need a wallet to contain:

- ◗ assessment information;
- ◗ current and preceding IEPs and review sheets;
- ◗ any other relevant paperwork.

The wallets should be filed in class order for easy retrieval and updated regularly. If and when it is necessary to transfer a pupil to another stage, the wallet can simply be transferred to the relevant drawer.

Assessment information

It is a good idea for you as the SENCo to make an informal assessment of each pupil at School Action. This gives you an opportunity to get to know each pupil, so that they are not just a name on a wallet in a filing cabinet. These assessment results will provide a starting point on which to base the IEP targets. A record sheet to record assessments year by year is important. This helps all concerned with the child to see if progress is being made.

P scales:
www.qca.org.uk/8798.html

For measuring pupil progress where the early levels of the National Curriculum provide inappropriate descriptions of pupil attainment, P scales are very useful. The P scales provide a framework for describing pupil attainment each year or at the end of a key stage when that child's attainment would in the past have been recorded as 'W'. The P scales also provide a context for determining targets in IEPs.

Current and preceding IEPs and review sheets
These need to be filed together and in order so they can be easily retrieved. The latest IEP should be at the front of the wallet.

Other paperwork
If the pupil has involvement with an outside professional, such as a speech and language therapist, there should be some associated documentation. Similarly, there may be information on any medical conditions the pupil may have.

Also kept in the pupil's wallet should be photocopies of any letters and invitations sent to the parents or carers by the LA or outside professionals.

Third drawer: School Action Plus and pupils with statements
Each pupil at School Action Plus should have a wallet exactly as described above for School Action, with additional assessments for School Action Plus. It is helpful if each School Action Plus wallet contains a list of people and external agencies involved with the child, together with their contact details. The list can be used at review time to check all involved have been invited, and it can be handy to have it pinned to the inside of the wallet cover.

Each pupil who has a statement needs a similar wallet (sometimes two) with copies of the statutory assessment and statement as well as all the additional paperwork gathered during the preceding stages of the SEN process. Again, it is helpful to have a list of involved parties and contact details; a copy of the timetable of support for the child is also useful.

Fourth drawer: SEN documents
This drawer should contain all the documents that are essential or useful for carrying out the SENCo role.

Official documents
These should include at least the following:

- *Special Educational Needs Code of Practice* (2002) This sets out principles, practices and procedures that schools must bear in mind when organising provision within the school. All schools and LAs need to demonstrate that they are fulfilling their statutory duty to have regard for the Code.
- *The SEN Toolkit*
- *Removing Barriers to Achievement: The government's strategy for SEN*

◗ *Every Child Matters: Change for children in schools*

◗ **The school's SEN policy and provision map** All schools must have an SEN policy, which ideally involves all teaching and non-teaching staff. The full policy document must be accessible to teachers, governors, parents, support staff and outside agencies working in the school. It is a good idea to produce a summary of the policy for parents, who may find the full policy somewhat daunting and hard to understand. All parents must also be informed by the governors in their annual report about the special needs provision. As we move more towards more SEN funding and resources being delegated to schools, the school is becoming more accountable in reassuring parents that they can be confident that a child with SEN is receiving the provision they need. A provision map stating interventions and additional and different support and strategies at each stage of the SEN Code of Practice may be useful.

◗ **The LA's policy** This sets out the expectations and particular procedures for SEN followed by the LA.

◗ **The LA's management file or handbook for SEN** A guide specially for SENCos.

◗ **The school's prospectus** This should contain a summary of special needs provision in the school.

A useful parent website: www.sutton.lincs.sch.uk/pages /community/parentguides/ special.html

◗ *Special Educational Needs: A guide for parents and carers* This guide, produced by the DfES, may be given to parents to explain the whole SEN process. Copies are available from the DfES publications centre, telephone: 0845 602260. There are also a number of useful websites for parents.

◗ **Relevant information from the local Parent Partnership.**

Other materials

There will be plenty of times when you need to check facts, revise your knowledge and skills or deliver INSET to teachers. If you have the relevant information to hand when such needs arise, it will save a lot of time and effort. It is useful, for example, to have information about medical conditions that are likely to be encountered in school. So it is worth collecting and adding to the information in your bottom drawer things like leaflets and articles cut from educational journals and magazines.

SENCo checklists

It is useful to keep a checklist of paperwork that needs to be completed at the end of term. A checklist for the annual review is also useful (see page 31).

End-of-term paperwork

◗ Are all new IEPs written?
◗ Have all IEPs and review papers been filed?
◗ Have IEPs been sent to parents?
◗ Have teachers put new IEP and review papers in the class file?
◗ Has all other relevant paperwork been filed?
◗ Is the SEN list updated and have appropriate changes been made?

The computer

This has become an invaluable piece of equipment for all SENCos. You need to have a computer available for all your SEN work – if possible a laptop, which means you can work anywhere in the school or, for that matter, anywhere! *Removing Barriers to Achievement* encourages the use of ICT to help lighten some of the administrative burden associated with the SENCo role:

> Many schools complain about SEN-related paperwork. But most paperwork can now be dealt with electronically. We will identify effective ICT solutions and encourage schools to use them wherever possible.

On the computer you can keep copies of documents as well as templates for almost all the associated paperwork, which can be filled in and adjusted as required. This may include:

- ❍ all the paperwork relating to reviews, including the annual review meeting agenda;
- ❍ IEP sheets;
- ❍ letters to parents;
- ❍ TA monitoring sheets;
- ❍ copies of all children's current IEP targets;
- ❍ pupils' targets sheets;
- ❍ the SEN policy;
- ❍ the graduated response provision map;
- ❍ SEN end-of-term and end-of-year checklists.

SEN resources

Resources should be kept together on shelves or in other suitable storage, in an accessible place for TAs and teachers. Ideally this would be in an area specifically for SEN. All staff need to know where they can find the resources and they should be made aware that these resources are only for use with children who require additional or different provision from the normal differentiated curriculum provided by the class teacher. Teachers of younger pupils may be tempted to use SEN resources such as phonics materials. The problem with this is that when these are provided for an older pupil identified as having a literacy problem a few years later, they may remember they were used in the Reception class – which won't do much for self-esteem!

Top tip

Survival tip
If possible, place photocopiable materials near to the photocopier. They are more likely to be put back in the correct place.

Photocopiable resources

Photocopiable materials should be kept together in plastic wallets and clearly labelled. The file should include resources for:

- fine-motor and handwriting skills;
- phonics;
- development of writing skills;
- reading high-frequency and medium-frequency words;
- comprehension and cloze procedure;
- spelling;
- numeracy:
  - addition and subtraction;
  - telling the time, shape, space and measures;
  - multiplication and division.

Support materials

It is a good idea to build up a set of books that TAs, parents and teachers may borrow.

There are numerous support materials on the market and it is useful to have copies of relevant catalogues. It is important to keep an inventory of all SEN resources and to make sure new resources are added to it. It is also a good idea to build up a set of books that TAs, parents and teachers may borrow. This mini-library should include books on all areas of special need, but in particular the following areas identified in *Removing Barriers to Achievement* should be included:

- autistic spectrum disorder (ASD);
- behavioural, emotional and social difficulties (BESD);
- speech, language and communication needs (SLCN);
- dyslexia;
- moderate learning difficulties (MLD).

Support materials to match learning styles

We access information in three main ways. When we receive information *visually*, it is through written and visual materials (e.g. books, diagrams, worksheets and videos). *Auditorily* we learn through speaking and listening activities (e.g. audio CDs, story tapes, opportunities for discussions in class) and *kinaesthetically* we learn by feeling and doing (e.g. practical activities, drama, role play, playing music). Most pupils have a preferred learning style and it is important to have a range of materials to match their different preferences. In our experience, most SEN pupils prefer to learn using a kinaesthetic approach, so you need to ensure you have a wide range of resources that meet this need. It is a good idea to carry out tests to discover the preferred learning style of SEN pupils. Alistair Smith's book *Accelerated Learning in the Classroom* provides a sample test for preferred learning style and a lot more information on the subject.

The teacher's SEN ring binder

Every teacher should be provided with an SEN ring binder. As well as keeping the SEN documents together for the teacher, the SEN ring binder can help you monitor what is going on in the classroom. By referring to the class ring binder, you can, for example, check that the assessment information and records are kept up to date, and that review meetings are arranged and taking place. (If, however, you have chosen one week in the term when all reviews at School Action are to take place, it's easier to see if a review has been missed.)

If teachers are aware that you will check regularly on this information, they are much more likely to give it their attention! You can also use the teacher's information to update your own records – it is important that the class information matches the central SEN records. The ring binders should include at least the following:

- current class SEN lists;
- the school SEN policy;
- blanks of letters to parents (unless you have templates on computers);
- Records of Concern;
- relevant assessment information;
- current IEPs.

You may wish to provide particular teachers with additional material relating to the needs of specific pupils. For example, a teacher supporting a pupil with attention deficit hyperactivity disorder (ADHD) would need to be given as much information as possible about the condition.

Teachers should be reminded that the SEN ring binder contains confidential information, so it should be available only to teaching staff.

Current class SEN lists

There should be a list recording the names and phases of every pupil in the class who has been identified as having SEN. In addition, there should be three separate lists, one for each phase, to identify the action taken by the school, with space to record review dates. Information concerning children's special needs should always be left for supply teachers. The class teacher must take responsibility for updating the information in the folders.

The school SEN policy

By including this, you make sure that every teacher, including any supply teacher who takes over the class for short periods of time, has immediate access to a copy of the policy. Alternatively, you could put the policy on the school's network, and make sure teachers know how to locate it. Having them read the policy on screen does cut down on photocopying.

Records of Concern (blank and completed forms)

The SEN file contains the Records of Concern for the children in that class, plus evidence collected for individual children in support of the concern. The teacher should give copies of the completed Record of Concern forms to the SENCo to keep in the folder in the SEN filing cabinet. This gives the SENCo some idea of the potential problems. The teacher's copy in the SEN ring binder will act as a reminder to the teacher to observe the pupil until a decision is made about whether to provide School Action.

Relevant assessment information

This is useful because it reminds the class teacher of the information on which the pupil's IEP is based. It should be regularly updated to show what progress is being made.

Current IEPs

It is of course important that the class teacher is aware of all the targets on the IEP so these can be incorporated into weekly planning.

The SENCo's survival kit

This is an essential piece of equipment in the SENCo's armoury. The 'survival kit' is simply a collection of items that you will need whenever and wherever you are actually working with children. Collect together in a suitable box or bag:

- buff paper (children with specific learning difficulties often find it easier to work on this);
- felt-tipped pens;
- plastic pouches to put children's work in to keep as evidence;
- coloured reading overlays in a variety of colours to help children with reading difficulties (the child needs to choose which colour makes the words clearer);
- reward stickers and stamps;
- a variety of pencils;
- pupil targets sheets;
- pupil review sheets;
- a list of high-frequency words;
- phonics cards;
- digit cards;
- small whiteboard and marker;
- highlighter pen;
- a pad of sticky notes;
- a crocodile ruler with handle;
- computer programs;
- Easi-Grip® scissors and/or dual control scissors.

The SENCo diary

This is another piece of essential equipment. It provides an overview of all the meetings that are taking place and helps to co-ordinate the whole system:

○ Visits from outside agencies can be written in. If the diary is kept in the school office, when an appointment is made by the secretary it can be written in. The school secretary can also look in the diary to check that rooms have been booked.

○ The week for reviews can be decided on and written in the diary during a staff meeting.

○ Meetings in the diary should also be passed on to the school secretary.

○ Important telephone numbers can be written in the front.

Time

Finally, however well organised you are, the amount of time allocated for you to do the administration and attend meetings is an all-important factor in your ability to survive and succeed as a SENCo. *The Code of Practice* makes the following recommendation for the time needed by the SENCo:

> SENCos require time for: planning and co-ordination away from the classroom, maintaining appropriate individual and whole school records of children at School Action and School Action Plus and those with Statements; teaching pupils with SEN; observing pupils in class without a teaching commitment; managing, supporting and training learning support assistants; liaising with colleagues and with early education settings and secondary schools.
>
> (Para. 5:33)

A block of time – a whole morning or afternoon or a full day – will be most effective in helping you to do the job. Every SENCo recognises, however, that the workload is not distributed evenly throughout the year. In an ideal world, you would organise your time so that you could save up non-contact time and use it at the busiest periods. It is therefore vital to think ahead to make efficient use of your SENCo time. Here is an example of how one SENCo, who was also a class teacher, made this work:

Time allowance for SENCo work: 38 days per year   **Time usually taken:** 2 half-days per week
Cover: known supply teachers

○ First two weeks in September, SENCo allocation not used – 2 days saved
○ Last two weeks in December, SENCo allocation not used – 2 days saved
○ First two weeks in January, SENCo allocation not used – 2 days saved
○ SATs week – 2 days saved
○ Last week of summer term: SENCo time saved
○ The saved time was used to take extra half-days when there were annual reviews, School Action Plus reviews and secondary transfers to complete. This meant that all the work was completed in school time.

Records for pupils placed at School Action

Name Date of birth	Date of first review	Outcome	Date of second review	Outcome	Date of third review	Outcome

Records for pupils placed at School Action Plus / with statements

Name Date of birth	Outside agency involved	Provision and support	Date of first review	Outcome	Date of second review	Outcome	Date of third review	Outcome

Chapter 6
INSET

The Code of Practice indicates that an important part of the SENCo's role is to provide training for all staff – teachers and TAs – to ensure their competent delivery of the SEN provision. To some degree, parents also require training to enable them to help their children reach the targets on their IEPs.

As SENCo, whatever you can do to help parents is an important part of your job.

Training parents and staff

For parents of SEN children, using some of the SENCo time to hold a coffee afternoon can be quite a good way to provide the help and advice they need. In this way you can meet informally and demonstrate some of the activities, resources and equipment that you use with their children. It also gives parents a chance to share their own expertise and to realise that others may be experiencing the same difficulties and feelings. As SENCo, whatever you can do to help parents is an important part of your job.

For staff, there are five main areas in which you will need to provide training:
- the school SEN policy and provision map;
- identification of pupils with SEN;
- clarification of the special needs roles – who does what;
- target setting for pupils with learning difficulties;
- SEN resources for pupils with learning difficulties.

The rest of this chapter offers some ideas and resources that will help you deliver effective training in each of these areas. Many SENCos do not relish the role of training staff, but all say that it gets better after the first time.

The SENCo cannot know everything. There are occasions when it is better to invite a professional to train the staff, and all will gain from their expertise. This kind of visit is particularly important when the school has a pupil with a particular type of difficulty – a pupil who has been diagnosed with an autistic spectrum disorder, for example. In such a case, all the staff – including the lunchtime supervisors – must be given training to deal with this particular child. Similarly, if you have a child with hearing loss, every member of staff needs to be taught some of the signs which they can use to communicate with the child. As we move increasingly towards inclusive schools, and more SEN funding and resources are delegated to mainstream schools, we are required to provide an inclusive education for children with various needs.

It is particularly important that you don't forget the training needs of the TAs, who are often on the front line. It is a good idea to ask at TA meetings what sort of training they feel they need. You then need to make sure that time is set aside for the TAs to be trained, as a group in school, by the outside professionals.

The training sessions

On pages 47–62 you will find a suggested programme plus handout material for a series of five staff training sessions. You may, of course, need to cover additional topics, according to the particular circumstances in your school.

One of the keys to a successful training session is careful preparation. It doesn't make for a smooth start if everyone starts arriving while you are trying to set things up. So check you have everything ready in the classroom where the session is taking place before everyone arrives. All the resources you will need for each session are listed at the beginning of the suggested programme, and material provided in this chapter is indicated with an asterisk. Some of this material is best used with a computer and projector or interactive whiteboard; some will be best as photocopied handouts.

Session 1 The SEN policy and school provision map

Time

Approximately one hour

Venue

A classroom, if possible with interactive whiteboard

Intended audience

All members of staff and the SEN governor

Resources

- ❍ Every member of staff to bring with them their own copy of the school SEN policy.
- ❍ You will also need a copy of the policy and a copy of the school provision map, which will probably be along the lines of the example on page 48. If possible, arrange to have this displayed on the whiteboard.

Purpose

To ensure that all staff are familiar with the contents of the SEN policy. The policy must:

- ❍ outline basic information about the school's SEN provision;
- ❍ provide information about the school's policy for the identification and assessment of and provision for pupils with SEN;
- ❍ provide information about the school's staffing policies and partnerships beyond school.

The policy should be subject to an annual review in which its effectiveness is explored in terms of the progress and attainment of pupils with special needs in the school. It is essential that the views of the staff are sought on this matter, and that they have a say in what changes are required. The policy should make it clear how children are identified, and this is an important area for discussion. Staff may feel that parts of the policy are confusing and should be expressed in a clearer fashion. However, it is the governing body and headteacher who are responsible for developing and reviewing the policy, and any suggested changes must meet with the approval of the governors. It is therefore a good idea to invite the SEN governor to these meetings concerning the policy. (All schools must have a named governor responsible for special needs.) If, as a result of the meeting, you decide that changes need to be made, then the SEN governor should take the ideas to the governing body to gain their approval. The policy must continue to meet the requirements of the Code of Practice.

Programme

① Decide which sections of the policy are suitable for whole-staff discussion. Read through these sections with the staff, with a brief discussion after each. If you have the policy displayed on the whiteboard, make any proposed changes on screen in a different colour. After the session you can review the changes made and add them to the policy following the governors' approval.

② Along with looking at the SEN policy, the staff should examine the provision map for the school's graduated response. Discuss what is provided at each stage and check that teachers are familiar with the provision. Do they feel there is anything not on the map that should be added?

③ You review the session with the school SEN governor and headteacher, and decide on any changes that are appropriate.

Provision map for children in Key Stages 1 and 2

Stage	Additional provision and Record of Concern — Number of children: 45	SEN: School Action — Number of children: 17	SEN: School Action Plus — Number of children: 10	SEN: Statement — Number of children: 3
Provision	Differentiated curriculum; Differentiated homework; Differentiated weekly spellings; Booster classes; Small-group work; Partner work; Partner support; Mixed-age classes; Sets in Years 1 and 2; Ruth Miskin Literacy in Reception and Years 1 and 2; VAK Learning/teaching styles; Brain Gym®; Speaking and listening programme; Partner talk; Assessment for learning WALT and WILF; Individual work for each child in the Foundation Stage; PSHE lessons to promote self-esteem; Huff and Puff lunchtime activities	Further differentiated curriculum; IEP targets; ICT programs, including Word Shark; Small-group work; Additional reading, maths, and phonic and spelling groups; Individual teaching sessions (10–15 mins.); Behaviour strategies; For Year 1 children, opportunities to return to Reception class for small-group activities (autumn term only); Different reading schemes; Homework time organised for after school; Individual reward systems; Visual prompts on table; Buff coloured paper; Coloured reading rulers	Physio programmes; Fine-motor programmes; ICT programs; Social skills group work; Speech and language programmes; RML group, mixed age; Individual behaviour programmes; Individual teaching sessions (minimum 30 mins.); Individual support in RM Literacy; Transition programme work, e.g. reading simple bus timetables; Early access to school each day for children with physical and behavioural needs; Individual support in PE; Homework diaries; Precision teaching; Individual reading; Access to personal hygiene support; Named person to talk about problems and learning successes; Reward systems; Handrails for physical needs; Laptops	Individual support in class; Small-group teaching; One-to-one support on school visits; Specific programmes based on IEP targets; Fine-motor skills programmes; Individual/statement objectives; ICT programs; Occasional withdrawal from class for individual work; Life skills; Individual health and sex education with parents present; Transitional programme involving extra visits to new school, following timetables, etc.; Social interaction programme for play and lunchtimes; Provision at the end of day for parents to pick up their child from inside school; Use of symbols to aid understanding; Mouse and keyboard skills; Specialist fine-motor resources; Visual timetables; Visual rewards
Use of resources	LSA support in small groups; Parent volunteers for reading and spelling	LSA support in small group in class; LSA support in small-group additional work; LSA support in individual work on IEP targets; SENCo individual work on IEP targets	LSA support in small groups; LSA individual support; Speech and language therapist support in school; LSA individual support for physical needs in swimming and PE; SENCo support; LA support from visiting professionals	Lunchtime and playtime supervision for social interaction; Outside agency teaching; Speech and language therapist; PE support; LSA support for specific subject areas; ICT programs; SENCo support; LA support from visiting professionals

Session 2 The identification of pupils with SEN

Time Approximately one hour

Venue A classroom, if possible with interactive whiteboard

Intended audience All teaching staff, including TAs. It may be expedient to invite the school governor who has responsibility for special needs.

Resources
- The summary of the special needs process, as shown on page 50. If possible, this should be displayed on the whiteboard or OHP.
- Blank copies of the Record of Concern, one for each person (from page 17)
- Handouts 1–3: Areas of special educational need

Purpose To equip teachers with the knowledge they need in order to identify which pupils should be acknowledged as a possible cause for concern, and at what stage such pupils may require School Action. It will also remind them of the areas mentioned in the Code of Practice and help them to be vigilant in identifying a need.

Programme
① Display and discuss the summary of the special needs process.
② Using the handouts, discuss each area of SEN as defined in the Code of Practice. Discuss at what point a child's difficulty becomes a problem – which would mean putting them at School Action.
③ Provide every member of staff with a blank Record of Concern, and invite them to fill in each area, using a pupil who is a cause for concern as an example. Get them to focus on the type of evidence they would require before deciding to place the pupil at School Action. Carrying out this activity in pairs promotes discussion.
④ Discuss the completed Records of Concern as a group, then show an authentic Record of Concern which has already been completed for a child in school. Go through the evidence for every area, and invite comments and questions from the staff. Ask the staff to think about specific pupils in their own class and decide which area or areas best describes their special needs.
⑤ Question time and close.

The special needs process

The special needs process: a graduated response of action and intervention

School Action

The SENCo will support the class teacher in gathering information and will help to co-ordinate the child's special educational provision, working with the child's teachers, the literacy and numeracy co-ordinators, the parents and the child.

School Action Plus

Teachers and SENCo are supported by specialists from outside the school.

Statutory assessment

The LA considers the need for a statutory assessment and, if appropriate, makes a multi-disciplinary assessment.

Statemented provision

The LA considers the results of the statutory assessment and, if appropriate, makes a statement of special educational needs and arranges, monitors and reviews provision.

Handout 1: Areas of special educational need

Cognition and learning

A General learning difficulties

- Low levels of attainment across the board in all form of assessment, including, for young children, baseline assessments.

- Difficulty in acquiring skills (notably literacy and numeracy) on which much other learning in school depends.

- Difficulty in dealing with abstract ideas and generalising from experience.

- A range of associated difficulties, notably in speech and language (particularly for younger children) and in social and emotional development.

B Specific learning difficulties

- Difficulties with fine or gross motor skills.

- Low attainment in one or more curriculum areas, particularly when this can be traced to difficulties in some aspects of underlying literacy and/or numeracy skills.

- Indications that the low attainment is not global; these might include: higher attainments in other curriculum areas which do not make demands on the areas of weakness, higher performance measures of reasoning or attainments in one mode of recording or presentation than in another (for instance better oral work than written work).

- Signs of frustration and low self-esteem, in some cases taking the form of behaviour difficulties.

- Evident difficulties in tasks involving specific abilities such as sequencing, organisation, or phonological or short-term abilities.

- In younger children particularly, language difficulties such as limited skills in verbal exchanges or in following instructions.

- Evident difficulties or delays in forming concepts, especially when information requires first-hand sensory experiences.

Behavioural, emotional and social difficulties

- Age-inappropriate behaviour or behaviour that seems socially inappropriate or strange.

- Behaviour which interferes with the learning of the pupil or their peers (e.g. persistent calling out in class, refusal to work, and persistent annoyance of peers).

- Signs of emotional turbulence (e.g. unusual tearfulness, withdrawal from social situations).

- Difficulties in forming and maintaining positive relationships (e.g. isolation from peers, aggressiveness to peers and adults).

Handout 2: Areas of special educational need

Communication and interaction difficulties

A Speech and language difficulties

These may be identified in the following ways:

- Problems with the production of speech.

- Difficulty in finding words and putting them together in meaningful and expressive language.

- Problems in communicating through speech and other forms of language.

- Difficulties and delays in understanding or responding to the verbal cues of others.

- Difficulties with the acquisition and expression of thoughts and ideas.

- Difficulty in understanding and using appropriate social language.

- Frustrations and anxieties resulting from a failure to communicate, possibly leading to apparent behavioural difficulties and deteriorating social and peer relationships.

B Autistic spectrum disorders

These are characterised by a triad of impairments in social relationships, social communication and imaginative thought. Look out for the following:

- Difficulties in attuning to social situations and responding to normal environmental cues.

- Evidence of emerging personal agendas which are increasingly not amenable to adult intervention.

- A tendency to withdraw from social situations and an increasing passivity and absence of initiative.

- Repressed, reduced or inappropriate interactions, extending to highly egocentric behaviour with an absence of awareness of the needs or emotions of others.

- Impaired use of language, either expressive or receptive; this may include odd intonation, literal interpretations and idiosyncratic phrases and may extend to more bizarre expressive forms and limited expression, reducing the potential for two-way communication.

- Limitation in expressive or creative peer activities, extending to obsessive or repetitive activities.

Handout 3: Areas of special educational need

Sensory and physical difficulties

A Hearing impairment

- Changes in certain areas of academic performance, such as deterioration in handwriting or other areas of academic performance, tonal changes in speech, progressive failure to respond to verbal cues or increasing requests for the repetition of instructions.

- Physical changes such as persistent discharge from the ears, tilting of the head to maximise verbal input, excessive efforts to focus on the teacher's face when instructions are being relayed.

- Signs of frustration with themselves or others, leading to emotional or behavioural problems not previously observed and for which there are no obvious causes.

B Visual impairment

- Deterioration in certain areas of academic performance; these might include deteriorating handwriting, slowness in copying from the board, increasingly asking for written instructions to be given verbally.

- Deterioration in other areas such as hand–eye co-ordination, excessive straining of the eyes to read the board, needing to be at the front of the group to look at television programmes or share in story/picture books.

- Progressive anxiety and tentativeness in certain physical activities suggesting that mobility is becoming impaired.

- Evidence of associated stress leading to withdrawn or frustrated behaviour.

C Physical and medical difficulties

Some children who experience physical and medical difficulties have no problems in accessing the curriculum and learning effectively. In these cases there is no evidence to suggest that they have a special educational need. Those pupils who have physical needs already identified or a medical diagnosis will need to be carefully monitored for their educational needs by the school.

Attention should be paid to the following:

- Evidence of difficulties in the other areas of special educational need as set out in the draft Code of Practice (2000).

- Impact of the physical or medical difficulty on the pupil's confidence, self-esteem, emotional stability or relationship with peers.

- Impact of the physical or medical difficulty on classroom performance (e.g. through drowsiness, lack of concentration, lack of motivation).

- Impact of the physical or medical difficulty on participation in curriculum activities.

Session 3 Clarification of the special needs roles

Time Approximately one hour

Venue A classroom, if possible with interactive whiteboard

Intended audience The staff and if possible the SEN governor

Resources
- A flipchart or whiteboard if the room does not have an interactive whiteboard
- Handouts 1 and 2: The role of the class teacher
- Handout 3: The role of the SENCo
- Handouts 4 and 5: Pupils with statements

Purpose To clarify the roles of all involved with the SEN process.

Programme
① Begin by discussing the process, as described in the Code, through which pupils are identified as having special educational needs.

② Invite the group to discuss, in twos and threes, what they see as their role regarding responsibility for special needs. (Hopefully they will not expect you as SENCo to be solely responsible!) Ensure that non-qualified teachers and new members of staff are with more experienced members.

③ Write up their comments on the whiteboard or flipchart.

④ Discuss the handouts on the role of the class teacher.

⑤ Return to the small groups to discuss what they think the SENCo does.

⑥ Write up comments on the whiteboard or flipchart.

⑦ Look together at the handout on the role of the SENCo.

⑧ Invite general discussion about the role of parents and look at the handouts for pupils with statements.

⑨ Repeat for the role of the pupil.

⑩ Briefly go through the role of the governing body.

⑪ Before closing, review teachers' roles at each stage of the Code of Practice.

Handout 1: The role of the class teacher

At School Action

- Makes initial identification of the pupil with special needs and, in consultation with the SENCo and the parents, offers the child support with School Action. (SENCo prepares file for filing cabinet.)

- Attends a meeting with the SENCo and the parents to discuss the school decision to initiate School Action. Explains to the parents that the curriculum will continue to be appropriately differentiated to meet the needs of their child, but in addition the pupil will benefit from having their own IEP, with specific targets to suit their needs.

- If the parents fail to respond to invitations to a meeting, sends out a letter to inform the parents of the decision to offer School Action. Gives a copy of this letter to the SENCo for the pupil's wallet and sends a copy of the IEP to the parents.

- Helps to devise the IEP with the SENCo, parents and pupil.

- Ensures that the IEP targets receive sufficient teaching time and resources for the pupil to be able to achieve them.

- Arranges dates of reviews and fills them in on the SENCo wall calendar. Sends out review invitations to the parents.

- Differentiates the curriculum in all subject areas, when appropriate.

- Monitors the progress of the pupil and regularly updates any assessments in the SEN ring binder.

- Informs the SENCo of any problems that arise between reviews.

- Attends reviews, whenever possible. Provides the SENCo with a report if unable to attend.

- Liaises informally with parents on their child's progress towards the targets.

- Maintains ongoing liaison with the pupil on progress; uses the pupil's targets sheet, signed by the pupil, as a form of contract.

TO37121

Handout 2: The role of the class teacher

At School Action Plus

○ Continues to support the pupil as in previous stages.

○ If the pupil is provided with the support of a TA, must provide a timetable. The TA should be involved in the planning and liaise with the teacher.

○ Ensures that the TA keeps record sheets of any work carried out with the pupil, and that copies of these sheets are placed in the teacher's SEN ring binder.

○ Attends review meetings.

○ Takes account of advice of outside professionals and of how this may affect all areas of the curriculum, for the benefit of the pupil.

For pupils with statements

When a pupil receives a statement, the procedure is similar to that for School Action Plus. The class teacher must also prepare a written report to present at the pupil's annual review meeting, and help the TA with the preparation of their report for the meeting.

Handout 3: The role of the SENCo

At School Action

- Conducts in-house informal assessment, specifically devised to investigate the needs of pupils with learning difficulties.

- Gathers additional information from the class teacher through discussion, test results and any other appropriate sources, and fills in relevant LA paperwork.

- Sets up the IEP with the class teacher, parents and pupil, using the information from the assessment to inform the IEP.

- Attends an initial meeting to discuss with the parents the decision to initiate School Action, and describes ways in which the parents may help their child at home.

- Provides the parents with a copy of the IEP and *Special Educational Needs: A guide for parents and carers.*

- Discusses the IEP with the pupil and helps them to complete a targets sheet (or the class teacher may perform this task).

- Monitors the pupil's progress by checking the teacher's SEN ring binder and observing the teacher's updating of record sheets. Further monitors progress at review meetings, when the IEP will be reviewed and new targets set (use updated assessment for target-setting information). The decision to remove the pupil from School Action or put them forward for School Action Plus will also be made at a review meeting.

At School Action Plus

- Meets with professionals and devises an IEP for the pupil based on their recommendations and also in co-operation with the class teacher and parents.

- Arranges subsequent review meetings.

- Decides, in agreement with the parent, teacher, outside agency, headteacher and governing body, if (following a period of being supported by School Action Plus) a pupil requires a statutory assessment. If so, it is usually the responsibility of the SENCo to fill in the paperwork, collect the evidence and apply to the LA for a decision.

For pupils with statements

- On behalf of the headteacher, ensures that all relevant people are invited to the pupil's annual review meeting, and that all those required to prepare a written report do so in the time specified.

- Ensures that a suitable room is available for the meeting and that the parents, in particular, are made to feel welcome in what can be a difficult situation for them.

- Following the review meeting, sends back to the LA the completed report, recommendations and paperwork in the specified time, proposing new targets for the pupil for the year, if appropriate.

Handout 4: Pupils with statements

Parents

- Agree to help their child at home with specified IEP targets when appropriate.

- Offer support and encouragement to their child; ensure that the child attends school regularly; support the child with any homework that may have been set; ensure that the child wears glasses if appropriate, and is equipped with any other resources necessary for progress in school.

- Attend the review meetings.

- Inform the class teacher of any problems that occur between the review meetings.

- Co-operate with any arrangements made with out-of-school professionals.

- Provide the class teacher and SENCo with all relevant information about issues that may be impeding the progress of the child.

- Take care of the child's physical needs: sufficient sleep, diet, clothing, regular health checks (if appropriate) and so on.

Pupils

- Must be involved with deciding targets on the IEP and sign their targets sheet.

- Should be invited to give views on their progress and what they would like to happen in the future.

- Should receive feedback after each review meeting, or attend if appropriate.

- Should be encouraged to see the IEP as a positive procedure.

- Should be offered all possible support to achieve the targets, through differentiation of the curriculum and the provision of appropriate resources and teaching strategies to cater for individual needs.

- May have to accept some responsibility if the IEP targets are not achieved.

- Has the benefit of extra teaching support from a TA, when available. It may also be appropriate to involve other pupils (e.g. with paired reading or precision teaching).

Handout 5: Pupils with statements

The governing body

◗ Ensures that provision is made for pupils with special educational needs and has regard for the Code of Practice when carrying out duties.

◗ Makes sure that a responsible person – the headteacher or a named governor – is told by the LA when a child has special educational needs, and that those needs are made known to all who are likely to teach the child.

◗ Ensures that teachers are aware of the importance of identifying and providing for children with special educational needs.

◗ Consults with the LA and others when that is in the interests of co-ordinated special educational provision in the local area as a whole.

◗ Reports each year to parents about the school's policy for children with special educational needs.

◗ Ensures that parents are notified of a decision by the school that SEN provision is being made for their child, and that they will be allowed to join in all school activities whenever that is practical and compatible with the efficient education of other children in the school and the efficient use of resources.

Session 4 Target setting and writing IEPs

Time

Approximately one hour

Venue

The staff room

Intended audience

All teaching staff and other staff new to the school since the last training on target setting; the SEN governor

Resources

- ❍ Flipchart or board
- ❍ Handout: Assessment results to identify IEP targets (page 61)
- ❍ Copies of blank IEPs of the type used in school – one for each person

Purpose

To demonstrate how to identify appropriate targets for pupils in order to produce SMART IEPs

Programme

① Look at the sample assessment on the handout and discuss the findings.

② Ask the staff to decide, in pairs, the four priorities that will form the targets on the IEP.

③ Take feedback from staff. Write the four agreed priorities on the board and discuss.

④ Now ask staff to devise an IEP based on the four areas of priority. Use the IEP format with which the staff are already familiar. Emphasise that the targets they set should be achievable within 12 weeks (the time when the review meeting is due) and that the targets should be SMART – Specific, Measurable, Achievable, Realistic and Time-related.

⑤ Compare and discuss IEPs.

⑥ Review the session before closing.

Because it is important to relate targets to resources available in school, this session relates directly to Session 5. Ask the teachers to keep their partially completed IEPs, or gather them in and keep them yourself until next time.

Assessment results to identify IEP targets

Area of difficulty: literacy

Name: Sarah

Class: KS1 Year 1

Sight vocabulary: 15/45 Reception words

Spelling: 7/45 Reception words

Phonic knowledge: Knows all initial phonemes, confuses **sh** and **ch**

Writing: Can write own first name but not surname

Handwriting: **c**-based letters formed incorrectly

Reading book: ORT Stage 2

Sarah enjoys looking at books and tells stories in her own words – by looking at the pictures she recognises a few key words.

Strengths

Sarah's gross-motor control is well developed. She enjoys PE and games and she is a happy child most of the time in school. She is making progress with maths.

Other areas of concern

Sarah finds it very difficult to concentrate during class discussions. She is easily distracted and will distract others.

Session 5 Resources

Time

Approximately one hour

Venue

Wherever the majority of resources are located in the school

Intended audience

All teaching staff

Resources

❍ All SEN resources including ICT

❍ Partially completed IEPs from Session 4

Purpose

To look at the resources available for children who need additional and different provision, to become familiar with them and discuss what other resources may be needed; to identify resources to match the targets set on the IEPs.

Programme

① Look at the range of resources available. Encourage staff who have used any resources to give feedback on their use.

② Identify resources that would help in achieving the targets on the IEPs.

③ Encourage staff to borrow the resources for use in their classrooms, and to return them to the correct place.

④ Close by reviewing the session and listing other resources needed.

Final thoughts

We hope this book has been helpful. If you carried out the initial evaluation of your situation suggested in Chapter 2, you may find it useful to devise a follow-up evaluation using some of the ideas in the book to help with forming your action plan. This may reveal there is absolutely nothing more you need to do, and that what you have gained by reading this book is reassurance that you are doing all you can. If so, be reassured!

On the other hand, your evaluation may reveal some gaps, and you may decide that some of the ideas and resources suggested here would be useful for you. Take your evaluation to your headteacher, and discuss what you need to do in order to take the SEN provision forward. This may be more time, additional funds, extra TAs, further training for you, more training for staff or supplementary resources. You may even decide that you need to reorganise your whole provision. Prioritise your needs and then over a period of time you can work through your action plan.

Completing your evaluation sheet regularly is a good way to monitor yourself and your progress in the role of SENCo. If shared with your headteacher and governors, it will also help them see how the SEN provision is developing and raise their awareness of what a really great job you are doing.

What is success?

At the centre of everything we do is the child. Pupils with SEN are particularly vulnerable and, in common with all other children, they deserve the very best we are able to provide. They need an environment where they feel safe and valued. They must be given opportunities to make a positive contribution to the school community, benefiting fully from the learning opportunities and social experiences available. If we can provide this, we will be successful in our SENCo role. And what is success?

> *The person is a success who has lived well,*
> *Laughed often and loved much:*
> *Who has gained the respect of intelligent people;*
> *Who leaves the world a better place than he found it,*
> *Whether by an improved idea, a perfect poem or a rescued soul.*

From the poem 'Success', by Robert Louis Stevenson

References

DfES Publications (2001) *The SEN Toolkit*

DfES Publications (2001) *Special Educational Needs: A guide for parents and carers*

DfES Publications (2002) *Special Educational Needs Code of Practice*

DfES Publications (2004) *Every Child Matters: Change for children*

DfES Publications (2004) *Every Child Matters: Change for children in school*

DfES Publications (2004) *Removing Barriers to Achievement: The government's strategy for SEN*

Smith, A. (1996) *Accelerated Learning in the Classroom*, Network Educational Press